I can use my unique voice

ATTRIBUTIONS
Interior Text Font: Jessycat
Interior Title Fonts: Baskerville
Illustrator: Katie Grayson
Editor: Robbie Grayson III

BOOK PUBLISHING INFORMATION
Traitmarker Media, LLC
www.traitmarkermedia.com
traitmarker@gmail.com

ISBN
Paperback: 979-8-3304-2662-1
Hardcover: 979-8-3304-2788-8

BOOK INDUSTRY STANDARDS AND COMMUNICATIONS (BISAC)
1) JUVENILE NONFICTION / General
2) JUVENILE NONFICTION/ Health & Daily Living / Physical Impairments
3) JUVENILE NONFICTION| Girls & Women

Dedication

To the unsung heroes who listen with their hearts.

This story is dedicated to those who speak through actions rather than words
and to everyone who understands that true communication often transcends
language. To the silent struggles and unspoken triumphs, may this tale shed
light on the beauty of finding one's voice in the quietest moments.

Special thanks to CUMI COOK BREWSTER, a retired educator
who believed in this book from day one. We greatly
appreciate you and other educators whose tireless work
with our children often goes unrecognized.

With heartfelt gratitude,
Tamara & McKenzie Tuckson

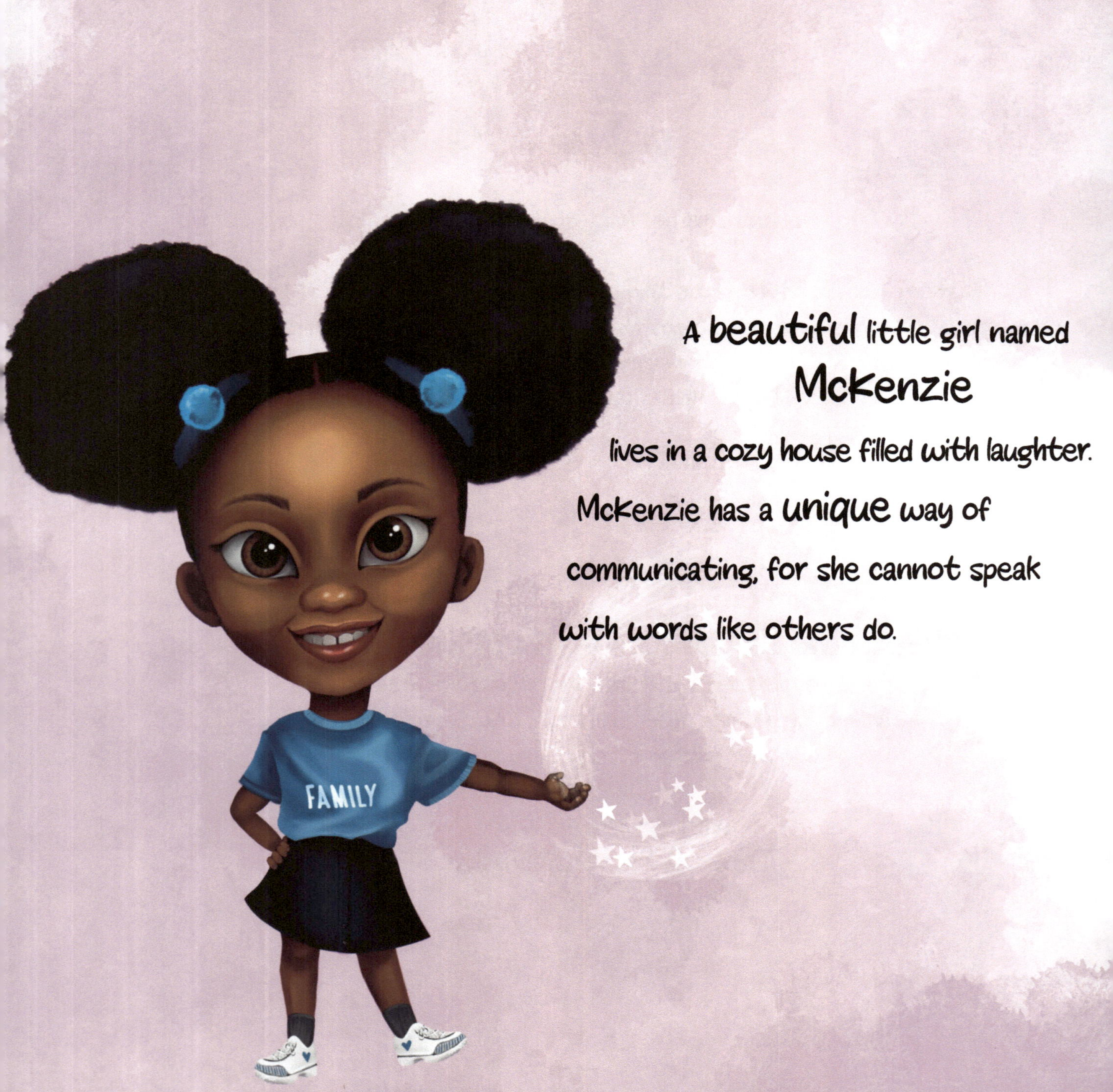

A **beautiful** little girl named
Mckenzie

lives in a cozy house filled with laughter.
Mckenzie has a UNIQUE way of
communicating, for she cannot speak
with words like others do.

DAD
MOM

Full of curiosity and concern, her cousins used to ask,

"Why can't McKenzie talk?"

They wondered if her voice was hidden or frozen in silence.

Where is your voice hiding?
Why don't you speak like us?
Is your voice frozen?
Believe
10

Advocate
Believe

With a knowing look at each other

and a gentle smile at the cousins,

McKenzie's mom and dad would explain,

"McKenzie has a unique voice.

She talks in her own special way."

HEY!

Mckenzie has a **magical** device called **PECS**, which stands for :

"Picture Exchange Communication System."

With PECS, she can choose pictures

to tell stories and share her feelings.

It is like painting with pictures!

As Mckenzie grows, her voice grows, too. She learns to use a device called **Tobii** that listens to her touch or understands her eye gaze. With this device, she can say: "I love you," "hello," and even share jokes that make her cousins giggle!

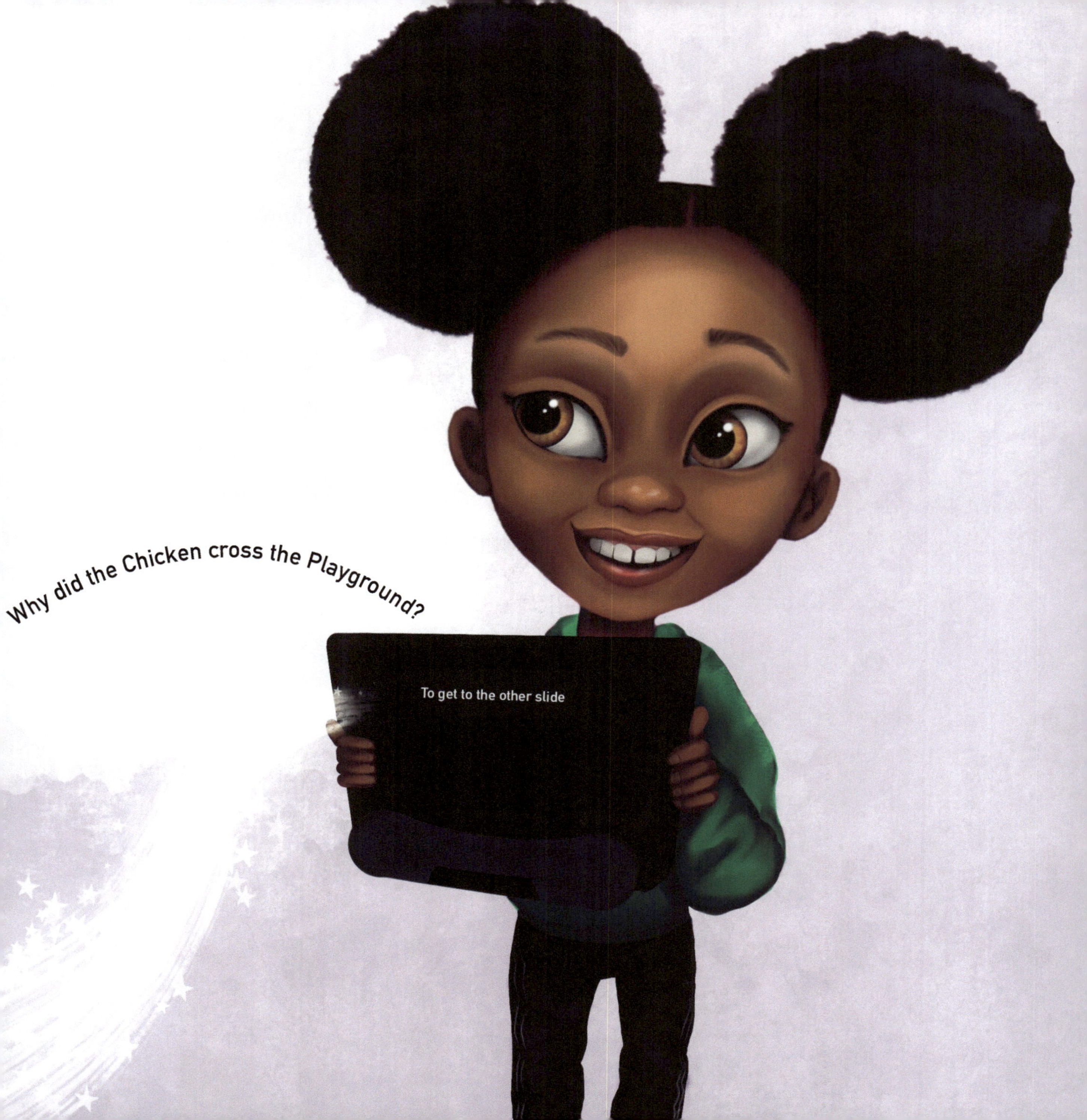
Why did the Chicken cross the Playground?
To get to the other slide

One sunny morning, McKenzie shows

her cousins how she can say a prayer

using a **Big Mack Switch**.

It is a special switch that lets her

speak with a tap of her finger.

Her cousins are in awe,

their eyes sparkling with wonder!

Faith

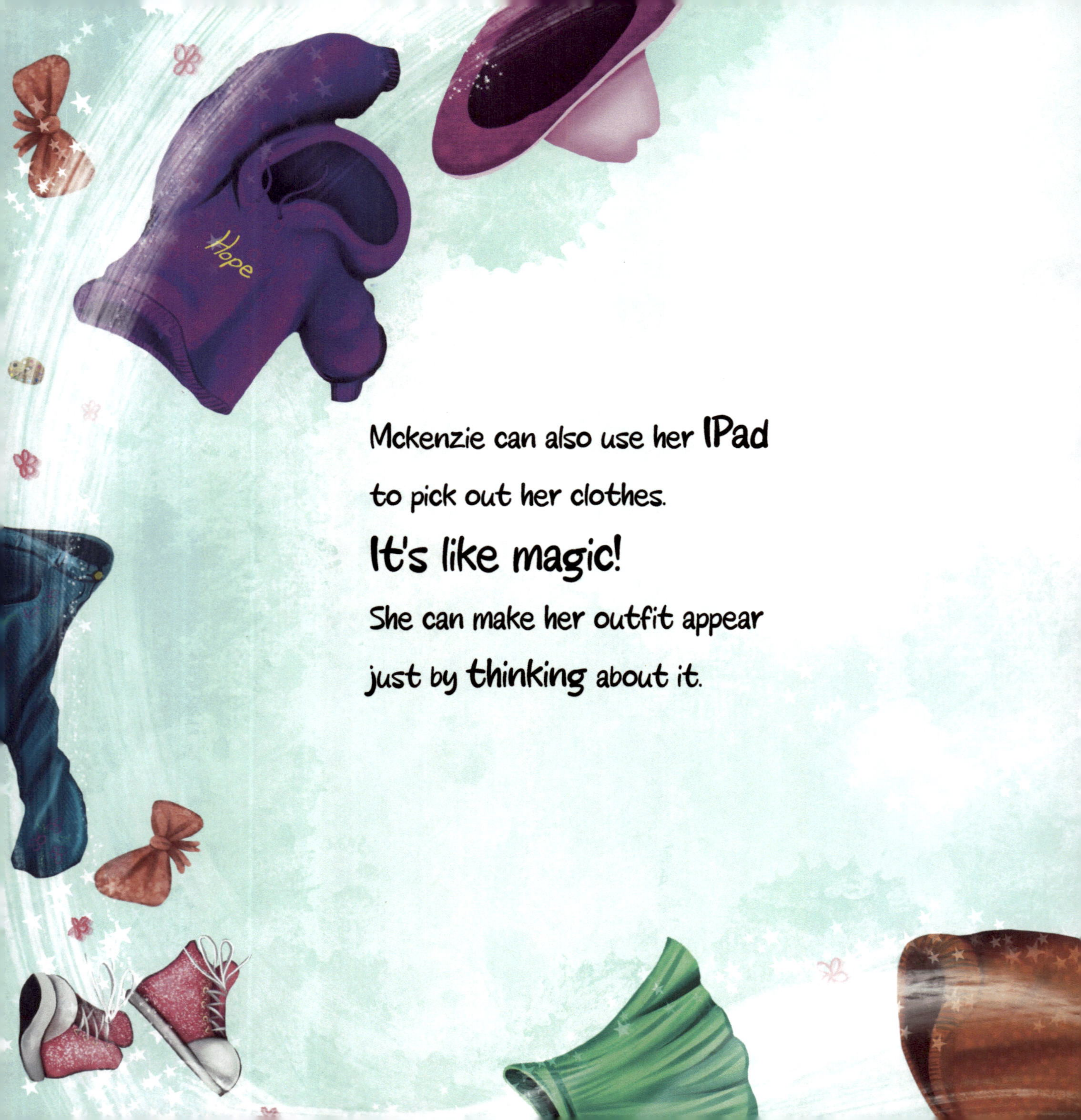

Mckenzie can also use her IPad

to pick out her clothes.

It's like magic!

She can make her outfit appear

just by thinking about it.

joy
FAMILY

LOVE
I love you! Happy Birthday!

Mckenzie's joy knows **no** bounds when she uses her **Tobii** to wish her Papa a happy birthday and tell him she loves him.

A **Tobii** is like a supercomputer that can read Mckenzie's **touch** and **eyes**.

Her heart dances happily, knowing she can share her love in **many** beautiful ways.

Mckenzie's grandparents are her
biggest cheerleaders.
They love spending time together,
sharing smiles and stories,
sometimes, without even saying a word.

Noel
Thank You

Christmas is one of Mckenzie's **favorite** holidays.

She helps pick out gifts for her family and shares

the excitement of decorating the tree.

When it's time to open presents, her eyes

light up with joy as she uses her device

to thank everyone for their

love and **thoughtfulness.**

Look what McKenzie made!

Her device helps her create **beautiful** artwork.

Every brushstroke is filled with color

and every piece tells her story.

Create

Mckenzie **loves** to dress up for Halloween!

When she is out Trick-or-Treating she wears her **Hipster** for on-the-go communication.

With this device she is a **SUPER** communicator!

Family karaoke night is always a blast!

Mckenzie joins in with her **Big Mack Switch,**

and together, they turn every song into a special memory.

BIRTHDAY
PRINCESS

Mckenzie's birthday is always the **best** day! With a little help from her device, Mckenzie makes a **wish** and blows out the candles.

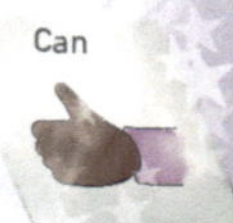

Now, when her cousins have questions,
they know they can ask Mckenzie **directly**.
She loves showing them the **many**
paths her voice can take.

Mckenzie's story reminds us that voices come in **all** forms,

and **each one** is a melody in the symphony of communication.

Just because someone can't talk the way you can

doesn't mean they have nothing to say.

With love and imagination, **every** voice can be heard.

Family

TAMARA TUCKSON is a passionate advocate and trailblazer for individuals with disabilities. Her advocacy journey began when her daughter McKenzie was diagnosed with Rett Syndrome. This rare genetic disorder inspired Tamara to transform her life's mission into a relentless pursuit of equality and justice. In 2015, she founded Mission2Advocate, an organization dedicated to empowering families by providing expert IEP consultation and support, helping them navigate the often daunting educational systems.

Tamara's impact goes beyond individual families; she has become a formidable voice in the broader disability community, participating in research studies and pushing for access to better therapies and treatments. Her tireless work to raise awareness and break down stigmas has made her a beacon of hope for countless families. Recognized for her unwavering dedication, Tamara received the prestigious Wayne Parker Advocate of the Year award in 2022. Her story is a testament to the power of a mother's love and her unyielding commitment to creating a more inclusive world. Through Mission2Advocate, Tamara inspires others to join her fight for a society where every individual, regardless of ability, can thrive.

MCKENZIE TUCKSON is not your typical 21-year-old; she is a dynamic and influential figure who redefines what it means to live with Rett Syndrome. Despite the challenges posed by this rare genetic disorder, McKenzie has become a symbol of resilience, breaking barriers and inspiring those around her. A varsity cheerleader with a keen sense of fashion and intelligence, McKenzie has made her mark as the first nonverbal Ambassador for Metro Nashville Public Schools and served as the President of both her junior and senior classes at Whites Creek High School.

Her leadership and advocacy work have not gone unnoticed; McKenzie has received numerous accolades, including the 2019 Westley-Rice Student Advocate of the Year award for Tennessee and the 2022 Westley Morgan Tennessee Titans Community Hero recognition. Beyond her public achievements, McKenzie is deeply committed to her faith, enjoys public speaking, and has worked at Bubble Love Tea for the past two years, demonstrating her independence and strong work ethic. McKenzie's journey is a powerful narrative of overcoming adversity and significantly impacting her community. She is a true trailblazer, redefining what it means to live with a disability and paving the way for greater inclusivity and understanding for all.

TO THE PARENT, GUARDIAN & TEACHER

Thank you for picking up *McKenzie Can Talk*. This book is more than just a story; it's a glimpse into the life of McKenzie Tuckson, a remarkable young woman with Rett Syndrome, a rare genetic disorder affecting her ability to speak. But as you have discovered, McKenzie's inability to speak does not define her—her strength, determination, and vibrant spirit do.

McKenzie's journey has not been an easy one. Like many students with disabilities, she has faced significant challenges in schools that are not always equipped to meet her unique needs. From inaccessible facilities to a lack of understanding about nonverbal communication, the obstacles McKenzie has encountered are, unfortunately, all too common for students with disabilities. These struggles often lead to feelings of isolation, frustration, and being misunderstood.

However, McKenzie's story is also one of hope, resilience, and the transformative power of inclusion. When schools, parents, and teachers make a concerted effort to include students like McKenzie—by understanding their needs, adapting learning environments, and fostering an atmosphere of acceptance and empathy—the results are extraordinary. Inclusion doesn't just benefit students with disabilities; it enriches the entire school community, teaching all students the values of empathy, diversity, and the strength found in differences.

As you read *McKenzie Can Talk* again and again, I encourage you to reflect on the takeaways that can make a difference in the lives of children with disabilities:

- **Understanding and Empathy:** Recognize that every child, regardless of their abilities, has unique strengths, emotions, and aspirations. Take the time to learn about their challenges and what you can do to support them.
- **Advocacy:** Whether you're a parent, guardian, or teacher, be a voice for children who cannot always speak for themselves. Advocate for better resources, more inclusive practices, and environments where every child can thrive.

- **Inclusion:** Embrace the importance of creating inclusive spaces. This means more than just Physical accessibility. It means fostering a culture of belonging where every child feels valued and included.

- **Adaptability:** Be willing to adapt your teaching methods, communication styles, and classroom environments to meet the needs of all students. Small changes can have a profound impact on a child's educational experience.

By embracing these principles, we can help ensure that students like McKenzie succeed and feel seen, heard, and valued for who they are. *McKenzie Can Talk* is a step toward building that understanding, and I hope it inspires you to make a positive difference in the life of a child with disabilities.

Thank you for taking the time to read and reflect on this important story.

Sincerely,

Tamara Tuckson (McKenzie's Mother)
Mission2Advocate

Resources

The following devices make it easier for nonverbal individuals to communicate effectively and gain independence. Scan the QR code to link directly to the manufacturer:

 **iPad Mini** | The iPad mini is a portable communication tool that works with AAC apps, helping nonverbal individuals express themselves easily. Its small size makes it convenient to carry and use anywhere.

 **Tobii Dynavox** | Tobii Dynavox uses eye-tracking technology to let nonverbal individuals communicate by controlling the device with their eyes, offering a hands-free way to interact with others.

 **Hip Talk Plus** | Hip Talk Plus is a wearable communication device that allows nonverbal users to press buttons to deliver pre-recorded messages, making communication easy while on the move.

 **Big Talk** | Big Talk is a simple device with large buttons that allow nonverbal individuals to play recorded messages by pressing them, making communication quick and easy.

 **Talkables** | Talkables offers customizable buttons for recording and playing messages, helping nonverbal users communicate simply and clearly by pressing colorful buttons.

 **"Say It Play It"** | This communication device helps nonverbal individuals communicate by pressing large, easy-to-use buttons. Users can record different messages for each button, allowing them to express their needs or thoughts quickly. It's lightweight, portable, and perfect for people with limited speech or motor skills.

 **PECS (Picture Exchange Communication System)** | PECS helps nonverbal individuals communicate by exchanging picture cards to show what they want or need, making it a helpful visual tool for both children and adults.

To contact the authors, order books in bulk, or
request consultations/speaking engagements,
go to **mission2advocate.com**